JULIUS
CAESAR
ROMAN GENERAL AND STATESMAN

SPECIAL LIVES IN HISTORY THAT BECOME

Signature LIVES

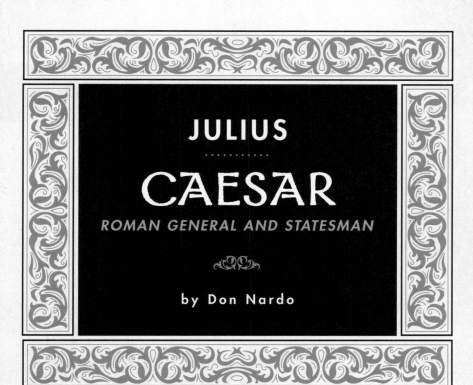

JULIUS
CAESAR
ROMAN GENERAL AND STATESMAN

by Don Nardo

Content Adviser: Josiah Osgood, Ph.D.,
Department of Classics,
Georgetown University

Reading Adviser: Rosemary G. Palmer, Ph.D.,
Department of Literacy, College of Education,
Boise State University

Compass Point Books ✦ Minneapolis, Minnesota

Compass Point Books
151 Good Counsel Drive
P.O. Box 669
Mankato, MN 56002-0669

Editor: Julie Gassman
Page Production: Bobbie Nuytten
Photo Researcher: Svetlana Zhurkin
Cartographer: XNR Productions, Inc.
Library Consultant: Kathleen Baxter

Art Director: LuAnn Ascheman-Adams
Creative Director: Keith Griffin
Editorial Director: Nick Healy
Managing Editor: Catherine Neitge

Library of Congress Cataloging-in-Publication Data
Nardo, Don, 1947–
  Julius Caesar: Roman general and statesman / by Don Nardo; content
adviser, Josiah Osgood; reading adviser, Rosemary G. Palmer.
    p. cm.
  Includes bibliographical references and index.
  ISBN 978-0-7565-3834-7 (library binding)
1. Caesar, Julius—Juvenile literature. 2. Generals—Rome—Biography—
Juvenile literature. 3. Heads of state—Rome—Biography—Juvenile
literature. 4. Rome—History—Republic, 265–30 B.C.—Juvenile literature.
I. Osgood, Josiah, 1974– II. Palmer, Rosemary Gudmundson. III. Title.
  DG261.N476 2008
  937'.05092—dc22
  [B]   2008005725

Visit Compass Point Books on the Internet at *www.compasspointbooks.com*
or e-mail your request to *custserv@compasspointbooks.com*

ANCIENT WORLD

Societies of long ago were peopled with unique men and women who would make their mark on the world. As we learn more and more about them, we continue to marvel at their accomplishments. We enjoy their works of art and literature. And we acknowledge that their beliefs, their actions, and their lives led to the world we know today. These men and women would make—and change—history.

Table of Contents

1 MIRACLE AT ALESIA

❧

The rising sun was beginning to burn away a thick blanket of mist. A wiry middle-aged man wearing a bright red cloak stepped out of the mist. Carefully he climbed a tower made of sturdy tree branches. His name was Gaius Julius Caesar, and he was in command of Roman troops in Gaul. Gaul was what the Romans called the region that today is France, Belgium, Netherlands, and part of Germany.

On this fateful morning in October 52 B.C., Caesar was preparing to fight a large force of Gauls. During the preceding six years, he and his men had conquered Gaul. But recently one of the Gallic tribes, the Arverni, had rebelled. They were led by their war chief, Vercingetorix. A tough, courageous, and clever military leader, he and his warriors had killed several hundred Romans. Caesar had spent months chasing them across the countryside. Eventually Vercingetorix and his warriors had occupied the fortress of Alesia, in north-central Gaul. Caesar had decided to attack Alesia.

The wooden tower on which Caesar stood was part of something much larger. It was one of many similar towers in a vast array of siege works (towers, walls, and moats) outside of Alesia. The Romans had long been known for their skills at siege warfare, which had helped them capture many forts and walled towns. Their planned assault on Alesia was a perfect example of putting those skills into practice.

Caesar's main goal was to keep the Gauls from escaping the fortress. He also wanted to prevent any reinforcements or food from getting in. So he ordered his soldiers to dig two deep pits, forming a double ring 10 miles (16 kilometers) around Alesia. More than 40,000 men labored on them for more than two weeks. They worked in shifts, day and night.

The people the Romans called Gauls were a branch of the Celts. Farmers and herders, the Celts occupied large areas of northern Europe in the centuries before Caesar's birth. Like other Celts, the Gauls were organized by tribes. They lacked the strong central political and military organization that Rome had. Also, unlike the Romans, the Celts had no written literature. For these reasons, the Romans considered the Celts savages.

In reality, the Celts were far from savage. Though they lacked cities and writings, they had laws. They also had complex social and religious customs.

Once finished, they tapped into a nearby river and filled one of the pits with water. It formed a vast circular moat. Then they collected the dirt they had dug from the pits and piled it up into a big circular mound. This artificial hill formed another giant, unbroken circle around Alesia. On top of the mound, Caesar's men built a palisade, a sturdy wooden fence. Every 82 feet (25 meters) along the palisade, they set up a tall guard tower.

The moat, palisade, and towers were not the only barriers blocking escape from Alesia. The Romans also covered the surrounding countryside with booby traps. Caesar later described one of the more deadly ones:

> *We dug pits three feet [91 centimeters] deep and tapering downward toward the bottom. Smooth stakes as thick as a man's thigh, hardened by fire and with sharp points, were fixed in these pits. ... [Each] pit was filled with twigs and brushwood so as to conceal the trap. These traps were set in groups, each of which contained*

Caesar's careful descriptions of the siege works make modern cross-section drawings of them quite accurate.

eight rows three feet apart. The men called them "lilies" from their resemblance to that flower.

Caesar could see most of these impressive siege works from atop the tower. He was confident that they could keep Vercingetorix inside the fortress. What worried him was what he saw when he looked in the other direction. The nearby open plain was alive with movement. More than 100,000 warriors had gathered to fight for Vercingetorix, who had become a hero to many surrounding Gallic tribes. The warriors' goal was to slaughter the Romans and liberate Alesia.

Caesar had expected Gallic reinforcements to arrive. So he had ordered his men to erect a second mound, palisade, and line of booby traps several hundred feet beyond the first line of defenses, facing the plain. The question was whether the outer defenses would hold against the enormous enemy forces. Caesar feared that his own troops would be attacked from both sides. Vercingetorix might assault

A skillful writer, Caesar kept a detailed personal log during his Gallic campaigns. In one section, he explains why he built the outer line of defenses around Alesia: "When [the inner] defenses were completed, I constructed another line of fortifications of the same kind, but this time facing the other way, against the enemy from the outside. These additional fortifications had a circuit of 13 miles [20.7 km]. ... My aim here was to make sure that, however large a force came against us, ... [we] could not be surrounded."

the inner siege works while the other Gauls pounded at the outer ones.

This frightening possibility soon became reality. Later that day the two-pronged Gallic attack began. The Romans were greatly outnumbered, and the Gauls must have thought their numbers gave them an overwhelming advantage. The attackers, Caesar later recalled, "felt sure that their own forces were getting the better of things." Also, "there were shouts and yells coming from all sides" as the Gauls "cheered their men on."

For a while it looked as though the Romans were doomed. However, their stout defenses and Caesar's

The fighting at Alesia was violent and bloody.

strong leadership skills were potent advantages. When the Gallic reinforcements tried to break the outer defenses, they died by the thousands. They "fell into the pits and impaled themselves [on the lilies]," Caesar remembered. Or they "were killed by ... spears shot at them from the rampart [a protective wall] and the towers. All along their line they suffered many casualties, but at no point did they break through our defenses."

At the same time, the Romans guarding the inner ring of defenses were successful. They were able to keep Vercingetorix from breaking through.

Seeing that his defensive lines were holding, Caesar launched a surprise counterattack. At his order, two groups of soldiers on horseback entered the fight. Caesar commanded one of the cavalry squadrons himself. "The enemy could see that I was coming," he recalled, "because of the scarlet [red] cloak which I always wore to mark me out in action." Hoping to kill the Roman commander, large numbers of Gauls "rushed into battle," he said. Meanwhile, the second Roman cavalry squadron attacked the enemy's rear lines. Most of the Gauls found themselves trapped and badly disorganized. Caesar said:

> *The enemy turned and ran. As they ran, the cavalry were upon them. There was a great slaughter. ... Out of all that great army, very few got safely back to camp.*

Caesar had turned almost certain defeat into victory. Many Romans viewed it as a military miracle. His tremendous victory at Alesia ended the great Gallic rebellion. It also completed his historic conquest of Gaul. Even before this feat, Caesar had been a major figure in Roman politics. Now he was one of the most powerful, and most feared, men in the known world. A cunning, resourceful general, he inspired almost blind loyalty among his soldiers. Two choices lay before him. He could voluntarily give up his military command and retire. Or he could use his army to try to gain ultimate power. Caesar chose the latter and set history on a dramatic new course. ❧

When it became clear that he could not win, Vercingetorix surrendered to Caesar.

B. CIVILETTI

2 A BRILLIANT REPUTATION

⚬⚬⚮⚬⚬

The strong leadership skills and sheer boldness that Julius Caesar displayed in the battle at Alesia were no fluke. These qualities marked his character throughout his adult life. He was also intelligent, proud, ambitious, and at times ruthless. He was a major gambler in the game of life. He took many calculated risks, some of which threatened to ruin or even kill him. Yet almost always he beat the odds and emerged the winner.

In addition, Caesar was a gifted writer. Fortunately for later generations, he left behind some long journals. These provide revealing glimpses into the mind of the most famous person Rome ever produced. Many other ancient authors wrote about Caesar. So his life and deeds are unusually well documented for someone who lived so long ago. This gave writers in later ages a lot of material to use in the many books and plays they wrote about him. The most famous is the play *Julius Caesar*, by the great 16th-century English playwright William Shakespeare.

Though Caesar's colorful life is well documented, the writings do have one major gap. Almost nothing certain is known about his childhood. Still, some facts about his family have survived, giving some idea of the conditions in which he was raised.

As a boy, Caesar had good reason for feeling proud of being a Roman. When he was born, on July 13, 100 B.C., Rome had the largest and strongest empire on Earth. The Romans controlled nearly all the lands bordering the Mediterranean Sea. And the

Julius Caesar is one of several plays Shakespeare wrote based on events in Roman history.

Roman army was both powerful and widely feared.

Caesar's family was well-known and respected by most Romans. His father, also named Gaius Julius Caesar, and through marriage, his mother, Aurelia, were members of Rome's old patrician class. The patricians were well-to-do, socially privileged, and politically powerful. They saw themselves as superior to the common people, or plebs. Patricians, along with newer noble families, controlled the chief ruling body of the Roman republic—the Senate.

Wealth and membership in the ruling class were not Caesar's only advantages as a youth. Several of his relatives were elected to high positions in the government. An uncle, Sextus Julius Caesar, served as consul, for instance. Rome had a republican, or representative, government, and the consuls were elected officials. The voters—freeborn adult males born in Italy of Roman families—chose two consuls annually. Advised and

In ancient Rome, a person's name indicated social status and family history. The first of Caesar's three names, Gaius, was his praenomen. This was roughly equivalent to a person's first name today. His second name, Julius, was his nomen, or clan name. His third name, Caesar, was his cognomen, or family name. It indicated which branch of the clan he belonged to. Thus Gaius Julius Caesar meant Gaius, of the Caesar family, of the Julii clan. Romans often left out the nomen when referring to one another, so he was commonly called Gaius Caesar. But thanks to Shakespeare's play, we call him Julius today.

overseen by the Senate, these high officials ran the government. The consuls also commanded the army during wartime.

Another of Caesar's uncles, Gaius Marius, served as consul a record seven times. Shortly before Caesar's birth, Marius gained a reputation as Rome's savior. Two large German tribes had threatened to overrun Italy, but Marius dealt them shattering defeats. Thereafter, he remained a towering figure in Roman politics. Growing up in his huge shadow, Caesar likely dreamed of being as famous as his uncle. But no one, not even Caesar, could have guessed that his reputation would one day surpass that of Marius.

As a general, Marius was celebrated and highly respected by his troops.

A comparison of the two men can be seen in one of the earliest documented events in Caesar's life. The year was 82 B.C., when he was 18. Caesar

received a message ordering him to report to Lucius Cornelius Sulla, the dictator of Rome. Normally the consuls appointed someone to serve as dictator only during a national emergency. The dictator ran the government in the consuls' place. He was expected to step down after serving for six months.

But Sulla's case was different. A powerful military commander, Sulla emerged as Marius' rival, and their forces clashed in bouts of civil war. Marius died in 86 B.C., but his supporters continued to oppose Sulla. In 83 B.C., after returning from a military campaign, Sulla took control of Rome by force. This was the first time a Roman general had ever done so. Then he made himself dictator and began harassing and murdering his political enemies.

Caesar was one of Sulla's enemies, partly because he was Marius' nephew. Also, Caesar had been an important member of Marius' political group, the *populares*. Sulla was the leader of an opposing group—the *optimates*. He had heard that Caesar

Lucius Cornelius Sulla (138–78 B.C.)

By the time he was in his mid-teens, Caesar was already an impressive-looking young man. According to the Roman historian Suetonius, Caesar was "tall, fair, and well built, with a rather broad face and keen, dark-brown eyes ... He was something of a dandy, always keeping his head carefully trimmed and ... having certain other hairy parts of his body plucked with tweezers."

had recently married a teenage girl named Cornelia. She was the daughter of the populares' leader, Cornelius Cinna. It was with Cornelia that Caesar had his first child. A daughter was born in about 83 B.C., and they named her Julia.

Cornelia was a central subject of the meeting between Sulla and Caesar. Sulla said he wanted Caesar to divorce her. It would be a public way for the young man to cut his ties with the populares. After that, the dictator insisted, Caesar would join the optimates. And any earlier "crimes" Caesar had committed against Sulla would be forgiven.

To Sulla's surprise, however, Caesar boldly refused to give up Cornelia. Furious, Sulla ordered that Caesar be arrested and executed, forcing the young man and his wife to go into hiding. Fortunately for them, Caesar's mother, Aurelia, had a cousin, named Aurelius Cotta, on Sulla's staff. Cotta pleaded with Sulla to spare Caesar. Eventually the dictator gave in. Sulla had looked Caesar in the eye and recognized a truly formidable foe. "Never forget," Sulla allegedly told Cotta, "that the man whom you want me to spare will one day prove the ruin of the party which you and I have so long defended. There are many Mariuses in this fellow Caesar."

Sulla did not live long enough to see his prophecy about Caesar come true. The dictator died unexpectedly in 78 B.C. For a while, Rome came back under the traditional rule of consuls, senators, and other republican officials.

This turn of events pleased Caesar. He could now devote his energies to making a name for himself in politics. He threw lavish dinner parties for Rome's

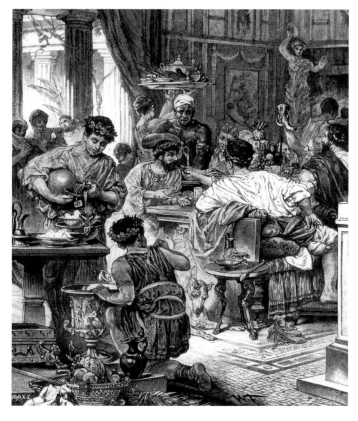

Roman dinner parties included rich foods and professional entertainment such as singing and dancing.

best-known citizens, hoping to impress them. He also worked to build the public image of a friend of common folk. Slyly, he recognized that he would need their votes in his future political campaigns. In this way, "Caesar won a brilliant reputation and great popularity," his ancient biographer, Plutarch, wrote.

> *He had an ability to make himself liked, which was remarkable in one of his age. And he was very much in the good graces of the ordinary citizen because of his easy manners and the friendly way in which he mixed with people. ... All this made him gradually more and more important politically.*

Caesar also built his reputation by giving long public speeches, the main way that leaders gained popularity. Caesar had excellent natural speaking skills. But he wanted to further improve them. So he traveled to the Greek island of Rhodes to study with a famous orator, Apollonius Molo.

On the way to Rhodes, Caesar was captured by pirates. For 40 days they held him prisoner while his servants gathered the ransom the pirates demanded. But Caesar showed no fear. As Plutarch reported, Caesar ordered the pirates to be quiet when he was sleeping. He also called them "illiterate savages and would laughingly threaten to have them all hanged," Plutarch wrote. The pirates thought Caesar was

joking, but he was not. As soon as he was free, he hired soldiers, rounded up his former captors, and made sure they were executed.

Caesar did not let his captors frighten him and made it clear that they angered him.

This event showed a side of Caesar's character that no one had yet seen. He was willing and able to use violence in a swift, cold, and efficient manner. Combined with his other skills, it made him a serious player in an increasingly deadly game. That game was Roman power politics. ☙

3 UP THE POLITICAL LADDER

❧⦿❧

Not long after his run-in with the pirates, Caesar began his slow but steady rise to ultimate power. He wanted major political success and military glory. Only a handful of men in each generation, he realized, managed to reach such heights. His uncle Marius and the dictator Sulla had been the towering figures of the last generation. Now Caesar, in his late 20s, had new role models in Pompey and Crassus. Gnaeus Pompeius, whom everyone called Pompey, was Rome's most popular general. Marcus Licinius Crassus was the richest man in the realm.

Caesar watched these two men become national heroes in 71 B.C. Two years earlier, some slaves had escaped from a gladiator school in a town south of Rome. They encouraged other slaves to join them.

When the government sent troops to put down the uprising, the slaves, under their resourceful leader, Spartacus, defeated them. Fear now spread through Italy that all Roman slaves would rebel and take up arms. Eager to gain a military reputation, Crassus offered to destroy the rebels. And he eventually did so, with Pompey's help. As a result, Pompey and Crassus became Rome's most powerful and influential men.

Spartacus is believed to have been killed in the battle against Crassus' army.

Caesar knew he could not compete with such renowned figures. He lacked the experience and public support they enjoyed. Roman tradition demanded

that young men seeking political power start at the bottom. A ladder of increasingly important public offices existed. It was called the *cursus honorum*, or "course of honors." Caesar realized that he must climb this ladder one step at a time.

The first step in the cursus honorum was service in the army. To meet this requirement, Caesar had been elected to the post of military tribune in 72 B.C. Each year the voters chose these junior army officers. A tribune's job was to carry out various tasks assigned by his legate. In Caesar's time, a legate was a commander of a legion, a unit of about 5,000 men. It is not known which legion Caesar served in. But he likely took part in the campaign against Spartacus' slave army.

Soon after completing his military service, Caesar faced a personal crisis. His wife Cornelia, then only around 27, died from unknown causes. That left the grief-stricken Caesar as the only parent of their 13-year-old daughter, Julia. Thereafter, Julia was likely cared for by

The army of the late Republic, which Caesar both served in and led, is sometimes called Rome's Marian army. It is named for Caesar's uncle, the great general Gaius Marius. In his years as consul, Marius completely overhauled the military. Before, its ranks had been dominated by citizens who owned property. He welcomed recruits from the poorer classes, too, and expanded and improved training. In addition, Marius ordered the troops to carry all their supplies on their backs rather than rely on mules. As a result, low-ranking Roman soldiers became known as "Marius' mules."

relatives and nursemaids, which was the custom.

At about this time, Caesar achieved the next step on Rome's political ladder. In 69 B.C. he was elected to the office of quaestor. The voters annually chose 20 quaestors, who acted as financial managers for the government and army. Caesar served his quaestorship in the province of Spain. The job thoroughly bored him, but he dutifully put in his time. He knew it was a necessary part of his long-term quest for power.

According to his ancient Greek biographer, Plutarch, Caesar spent large sums of money while serving as aedile, in large part to promote his image among the people. "He spent money recklessly, and many people thought that he was purchasing a moment's brief fame at an enormous price, whereas in reality he was buying the greatest place in the world at inconsiderable [minor] expense." In one case, Caesar was in charge of the building of the Appian Way, a major Roman road. In addition to the budget supplied by the government, Caesar gave a large amount of his own money to the project.

More determined than ever to achieve his goals, Caesar returned to Rome by 67 B.C. The next step in the cursus honorum, he knew, was the office of aedile. Four aediles were elected each year. Their job was to maintain public buildings and supervise public markets, festivals, and games. Their efforts were highly visible to all citizens. And Caesar realized that pleasing the public could make him a household name. That would give him more political power.

To make sure he was success-

ful as an aedile, Caesar planned to spend some of his own money on public entertainments. Though he was already well-to-do, it seemed wise to acquire still more wealth. He married a young woman named Pompeia, who was from one of Rome's richest families. Caesar was not in love with Pompeia, but he had much to gain from this marriage. Not only did Pompeia come from wealth, she was Sulla's

Rome had a simple but thriving economy, so Caesar's position as aedile easily put him in the public eye.

granddaughter. This gave Caesar a chance to gain friends and supporters among the optimates, which might further aid his career.

That career reached a new level when Caesar was elected aedile in 66 B.C. During his term, served in the following year, "he spent money recklessly," as Plutarch put it. In one episode, Caesar had artists create several beautiful statues of Marius and the goddess Victory. He placed them in a prominent place in Rome. "And all who saw them were amazed at the daring of the man who had set them up," Plutarch wrote.

Caesar also spent some of his own money to stage the most lavish gladiator battles Rome had yet witnessed. "He provided a show of 320 pairs of gladiators fighting in single combat," Plutarch said. It was so popular, wrote the biographer, "that every man among them [the public] was trying to find new offices and new honors to bestow upon him."

Among these new offices and honors was the next rung on the traditional political ladder—praetor. Caesar won election to this post in 63 B.C. Eight praetors were elected each year to serve as high court judges. The job was seen as prestigious. Another benefit was that after serving their terms, many praetors were appointed provincial governors. Governors had access to large amounts of

public money and legions of troops. Caesar wanted to get his hands on both.

The year 63 B.C. also proved pivotal for Caesar because of two events he did not expect. First, the daughter of one of his sisters gave birth to a child. The boy's name was Gaius Octavius, but he is more commonly known today as Octavian. At the time, no one, including Caesar, suspected that the boy would later become Caesar's heir and one of the towering figures of Roman history.

At the end of a gladiator battle, the victor would look to the crowd to see whether he should spare his opponent. A thumbs down signaled that the defeated man should be killed.

Also in 63 B.C., Caesar suddenly found himself playing an important role in a national emergency. Along with other Roman leaders, he heard that a group of conspirators was planning a coup.

In the same year he won election as praetor—63 B.C.— Caesar achieved another important public office. Roman voters chose him as pontifex maximus, chief priest of the state religion, a position that was not part of the cursus honorum. It was not a full-time job, and the man who held it was free to pursue other political or military offices. The chief priest consecrated, or made holy, new temples and regulated the public calendar. He also made or upheld laws relating to burial and performed other religious duties. Caesar held the post until his death.

The ringleader—Lucius Sergius Catilina, known as Catiline— wanted to murder the consuls and take over the government.

The plot failed, and Catiline and some of his followers were captured. Some Roman leaders demanded that they be immediately executed, without benefit of a trial. Others, including Caesar, pointed out that this was a violation of Roman law. In a dramatic speech to the Senate, he delivered a warning: Those who advocated ignoring the law risked harming their reputations in the long run. But most senators disagreed and voted to execute Catiline and his followers.

Though Caesar's words were ignored, in time they rang true. Public opinion eventually turned against the Senate for its violation of established law and tradition.

In contrast, Caesar looked like a man of wisdom and principle. He hoped this would help him in his next, and toughest, political contest so far—a fight for the consulship. ✍

The noted orator Cicero, who was a consul, gave a speech against Catiline in the Senate.

4

THE CORRIDORS OF POWER

❧⚬✕⚬❧

After serving as praetor in 62 B.C., Julius Caesar was eager to be appointed governor of one of Rome's provinces. Provincial governors were powerful and important figures. Each presided over thousands of square miles of territory and hundreds of thousands of people. In addition, a governor was in command of the thousands of Roman troops stationed in his province and could use them for military campaigns.

Caesar knew that leading successful military campaigns was the only way to acquire the level of fame and power he desired. Rumors said the Senate was going to grant him the governorship of Spain. Large groups of bandits were terrorizing Roman towns in the western part of the country. Caesar dreamed of defeating these criminals and receiving the honor of a splendid parade known as a triumph. During a triumph, a victorious general drove a ceremonial chariot, with his troops marching with him.

Early in 61 B.C., after acquiring the Spanish province, Caesar prepared for the journey there. Shortly before his ship set sail, however, he encountered trouble. Though he was well-to-do, he often spent more money than he made. And he had recently borrowed to make up a shortfall. Perhaps, he thought, he could acquire slaves in Spain and sell them to make money to pay off his debts. At the moment, however, his creditors were threatening to seize his luggage if he did not pay them. "He therefore turned for help to Crassus," Plutarch wrote, "who was the richest man in Rome and who needed Caesar's vigour and fire for carrying out his own political campaign." Crassus gladly paid off the creditors, and Caesar was free to leave on his journey.

Marcus Licinius Crassus (115–53 B.C.)

Arriving in Spain three weeks later, Caesar wasted no time in putting his plan into action. He took command of the province's 10,000 troops and swiftly gathered another 5,000. Then he went after the bandits and defeated them. His soldiers became extremely devoted to him. They saw Caesar as a gifted manager and brilliant military leader. The experience of commanding an army in battle fascinated and thrilled him. His modern biographer, Michael Grant, puts it well: "It showed him what he did best: and what he best liked to do."

Having achieved success in Spain, in June 60 B.C., Caesar returned to Rome, leaving his governorship and army behind. He naturally looked forward to taking part in his triumph. Visions of huge crowds cheering him as a conquering hero filled his head.

However, a serious legal problem soon threatened to dash these dreams. Caesar desperately wanted to run for consul, the highest political post in Rome. The elections for the consulship of the following year, 59 B.C., were to be held in just a few weeks. It was vital that he begin campaigning immediately, but there was an obstacle. According to Roman law, a general who

Military triumphs were grand, colorful ceremonies in ancient Rome. The general who was being honored rode in a beautifully decorated chariot. His troops marched either behind or in front of him. Some of the soldiers carried statues, gold, and other loot taken during the campaign. Other troops led captured enemies, who wore shackles and chains. The triumphant general was clad in a purple toga and wore laurel leaves in his hair.

had been granted a triumph could not enter Rome before the ceremony.

Desperate, Caesar asked the Senate to allow him to run for consul *in absentia*, or "in his absence." In this arrangement, one of his friends would make political speeches for him. To Caesar's disappointment, however, the senators refused his request. The refusal was mainly the work of the leading optimates. They wanted to keep Caesar and other important populares from gaining too much power and influence.

Caesar had to choose between enjoying his military triumph and running for consul. Reluctantly, he opted to give up his triumph. Feeling bitter and angry, he hatched a plan to strike back at his political opponents. Shortly before the consular elections, Caesar approached both Crassus and Pompey in secret. He proposed that the three of them form an alliance. Alone, he argued, each lacked the power and influence to successfully oppose the optimates and Senate. But together, they might be able to do so.

Crassus and Pompey did not like or trust each other. Each was also wary of Caesar and his ambitions. Like Caesar, however, they saw the potential of pooling their considerable resources. Thus was born an informal alliance that is known today as the First Triumvirate. (The term *triumvirate* was roughly defined as "rule of the three." It came

from an old Latin phrase, *trium virorum,* meaning "of three men.")

The combined efforts of the three men—the triumvirs—was highly effective. Backed by Pompey's and Crassus' supporters, as well as his own, Caesar easily won one of the consular posts. A politician named Marcus Bibulus was also elected consul, filling the second position. Bibulus was backed by the optimates. They hoped he would be able to keep Caesar's power in check.

However, Bibulus was a timid man with limited talents. It quickly became obvious that he could not stand up to the triumvirs. When Caesar proposed a bill intended to grant plots of land to Pompey's retired soldiers, Bibulus and a leading senator, Marcus Cato, tried to speak against the bill in the voters' assembly. But Caesar had allowed Pompey to bring some of his soldiers to the meeting. These armed men drove Bibulus and Cato away. According to Plutarch, Bibulus was so upset and fearful "that he stayed at home for the rest of his term." Caesar was able "to govern alone

When Bibulus opposed Caesar, he was silenced by a mob of Caesar's supporters.

and do very much as he pleased."

And so it went. Caesar's entire year as consul was marked by corruption and shady dealings. Using bribes and bully tactics, the triumvirs largely silenced the opposition. As a result, they were able to over-shadow the government.

Caesar also wisely strength-ened his ties to one of his partners. He arranged for his daughter Julia, then about 23, to marry Pompey, who was a bit more than twice her age. For Caesar, this move was largely a means to an end. Good relations with Pompey were essential because Caesar needed Pompey's troops to enforce his policies.

Caesar's daughter, Julia (83–54 B.C.)

But Ceasar realized he could not rely on Pompey forever. To continue his climb through the corridors of power, Caesar had to build his own loyal army. The only practical way to do so was to get his hands on another province. ❧

5 THE CONQUEST OF GAUL

ᥫᨆᨆᥣ

With his year as consul almost at an end, Julius Caesar thought about his future and considered his options. If he retired to private life, he would lose most of his power. Also, his enemies might try to take him to trial for his corrupt dealings as consul.

Becoming governor of another province was far more attractive. First and foremost, he would remain a powerful figure in Roman affairs. With an army at his disposal, he could continue to wield influence and build his reputation. Another benefit of obtaining a governorship was the legal protection it offered. Roman law forbade the prosecution of a sitting governor, consul, or other high official for offenses in the past.

Normally the Senate awarded outgoing consuls

their provinces. Knowing that most of the senators despised him, Caesar simply bypassed them. He got the voters in the assembly to pass a special law granting him a province. It consisted of two neighboring regions. The first was Cisalpine Gaul, in the extreme northern part of Italy. The other was Illyricum, a coastal strip on the far side of the Adriatic Sea, facing eastern Italy. This gave Caesar control of three legions—more than 15,000 troops. Moreover, he was given the governorship for five years instead of the usual one.

Shortly before leaving Rome for his province, Caesar received an unexpected bonus. The Roman politician who was supposed to become governor of Narbonese Gaul unexpectedly died. Usually referred to simply as the Narbonese (or Narbonensis), the province included what is now southern France. Caesar's father-in-law, Calpurnius Piso, persuaded the Senate and voters to add the Narbonese to Caesar's other province. That brought a fourth legion under Caesar's command. He could barely contain his excitement about his good luck. According to one ancient source, he boasted to the Senate that he had "gained his dearest wish, to the annoyance

At about the same time that Pompey and Julia wed, her father also took a new wife. Caesar had divorced Pompeia in 62 B.C. His new bride was Calpurnia, daughter of Calpurnius Piso. A wealthy former provincial governor, Piso openly supported Caesar when Caesar was consul. Once again, Caesar was marrying for convenience rather than love.

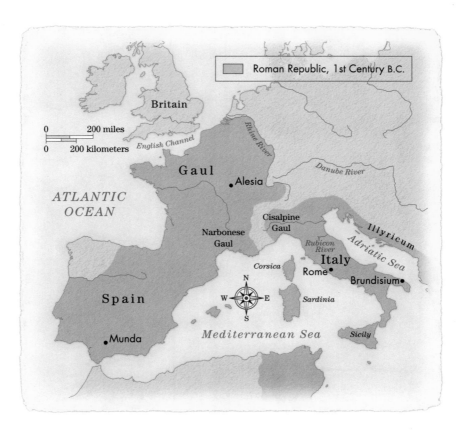

Roman Republic, 1st Century B.C.

Britain

0   200 miles
0   200 kilometers   *English Channel*

Rhine River

Gaul   •Alesia

Danube River

ATLANTIC
OCEAN

Cisalpine
Gaul

Narbonese
Gaul

Illyricum

*Rubicon
River*

Adriatic Sea

Corsica   Italy
Rome•
Brundisium•

Spain

N
W   E
S

Sardinia

•Munda   *Mediterranean Sea*   *Sicily*

*The regions
of Caesar's
provinces
were several
hundred
miles apart.*

and grief of his opponents."

Caesar departed for his Gallic provinces early in 58 B.C. Administering them was clearly going to be a major task. Yet already he had an even bigger goal in mind. North and west of the Narbonese lay an area known to Rome as Transalpine Gaul. It consisted of what are now central and northern France, Belgium, Netherlands, and parts of Switzerland. The Romans had no clear idea of the region's size and extent. Nor did they know the number and size of

Gallic men often wore their hair long and dressed in furs. The Romans considered the men to be barbarians.

the Gallic tribes that lived in the area.

Caesar hoped to learn these facts and conquer the peoples of the region. This would surely bring him great fame and power. To make sure the Roman people knew about his adventures, he kept a journal.

And as he wrote new installments, messengers carried them to Rome. Eventually they were published and widely read.

The first major adventure Caesar described was a campaign against the Helvetii. This Gallic tribe hailed from what is now northern Switzerland. German tribesmen who lived east of the Rhine River were harassing the Helvetii. So the Helvetii decided to abandon their villages and migrate westward. Caesar realized that their march would take them through the Narbonese. This gave him an excuse to attack them and thereby launch his Gallic conquests.

Hastily moving his troops, Caesar encountered the Helvetii not far north of the Narbonese. Messengers from the tribe told Caesar they were just passing through the area. They claimed they had no intention of settling in Roman lands. But Caesar ignored them. He ordered his troops to attack the tribe's members as they were crossing a river. He wrote:

Caesar opened his famous journal, the Gallic Commentaries, *with a general description of the main tribal groups in the region:* "The country of Gaul consists of three separate parts, one of which is inhabited by the Belgae, one by the Aquitani, and one by the people whom we call 'Gauls' but who also are known in their own language as 'Celts.' These three peoples differ from one another in language, customs, and laws. ... The toughest soldiers come from the Belgae. This is because they are farthest away from the culture and civilized way of life of the Roman province [the Narbonese].

Since Germans were harassing the Helvetii, they sought a new, spacious area for their growing tribe.

Hurling their javelins from above, our men easily broke up the enemy's mass formation ... [then] drew their swords and charged. ... The wounds and the toil of battle were too much for [the Gauls] and they began to retire. ... It was a long fight, but in the end we gained possession of the [enemy's] baggage and camp. ... The Helvetii had now no supplies of any kind and could therefore do nothing except ... discuss terms of surrender.

It is not known how many of the Helvetii the Romans killed. Caesar claimed it was 258,000. However, he always exaggerated the numbers of enemy dead to make himself look more fearsome. Modern historians estimate that closer to 60,000 Helvetii died—still a horrendous death toll. Similar numbers of Gauls were slaughtered in Caesar's later battles with other Gallic tribes.

Among the other Gauls who opposed the Roman conquest were the Belgic tribes. They lived in the northern reaches of Transalpine Gaul. Because the various branches of the tribes were separate, Caesar's job was easier. He was able to fight and defeat them one at a time, beginning in the summer of 57 B.C.

By the end of that year, Caesar felt that major operations in Gaul were over. Some leading Gallic tribes had been impressed, even awed, by his victories. So they offered to sign treaties with him rather than fight. The strongest tribe of central Gaul—the Aedui—even became Roman allies.

It appeared safe, therefore, for Caesar to pursue military adventures elsewhere. He had been considering an invasion of Britain. The Romans then viewed this as a mysterious faraway land. Supposedly it

Of the Belgic tribes that opposed Caesar, the most difficult to subdue was the Nervii. Caesar described its members this way: "No traders ever came into their country because they did not allow wine to be imported or any other luxury, in the belief that indulgences of this sort make men feeble-spirited and lacking in courage. A fierce people and extremely courageous, they ... declared that they would never send envoys to us and never accept any kind of peace."

contained vast supplies of gold, tin, and pearls. Hoping to find these riches, Caesar led an army across the English Channel in July 55 B.C. But a storm wrecked many of his ships, and he had to abort the mission. He tried again the following year and got a little farther inland. Eventually, however, storms and other factors again forced him to turn back.

Returning to Gaul, Caesar was greeted by two pieces of bad news. His daughter Julia had died in childbirth. The baby, Pompey's son, had died, too. Also, the Belgic tribes had launched a rebellion.

Caesar managed to defeat them, but then farther south, the Arverni, led by Vercingetorix, revolted as well. It took Caesar until the end of 51 B.C. to bring all of Gaul back under his control.

In the course of seven years, Caesar had captured more than 800 towns and killed perhaps a million people. These feats had greatly expanded Roman rule. Caesar had become very rich from all the plunder and slaves he had acquired. This made it easier for him to bribe key supporters back in Rome. In addition, the Gallic conquests had made Caesar a legendary figure. Surely, he thought, when he returned to Rome this time no one would dare to deny him his triumph. But he was wrong. New battles, even larger and more fateful than those he had already fought, awaited him. ❧

Chapter

6 ENGULFED IN CIVIL WAR

‹⌒⌒›

Julius Caesar left the Narbonese and reached Cisalpine Gaul in 50 B.C. For the moment, he chose not to go on to Rome. His supporters and spies had long kept him informed of what was happening there. And at the time, they said, the situation was tense and dangerous for him. The era of the First Triumvirate was over. Crassus had died three years earlier during a military campaign, and the leading optimates in Rome had turned Pompey against Caesar.

Another problem was that it was no longer legal for Caesar to lead an army. His term as governor was ending and by law he was now supposed to disband his army. Also, he could not travel to Rome at the head of an army. By both law and custom, that would be seen as an armed attack on the state. And Pompey's

After his return from Gaul, Caesar wrote about some of his later adventures.

troops would surely resist, igniting a civil war.

But in Caesar's mind, going back to Rome without his troops was not an option. The Senate might order his arrest for his past offenses. Only after his election to another high public office would the law protect him from prosecution. So Caesar remained in his province for a while. Perhaps, he hoped, he could work out a deal with his political enemies.

The deal Caesar had in mind involved his running for consul again. He wanted to campaign in the July 49 B.C. elections. But that was not possible because he could not return to Rome. As he had before, he considered running in absentia. When it looked as if the Senate would not allow it, he turned to his leading supporters. They got the citizen assembly to pass a special law that would let others campaign for him.

But with Pompey now backing the optimates, they feared Caesar less than they had in the past. They said they would not honor the new in-absentia law. They even felt bold enough to try forcing Caesar into a corner. In December 50 B.C., the Senate sternly ordered him to give up command of his army. When he refused, the senators declared that he was no longer a governor. He told his soldiers: "Decrees of the most savage and ... insulting kind were passed, depriving me of my command." In response, he wrote, the troops "shouted out that they were ready to protect their general ... from injury and injustice."

The great affection and loyalty Caesar's troops felt for him filled him with confidence. He decided not to back down. On January 10, 49 B.C., he and his men marched to the Rubicon River. It marked the boundary between Cisapline Gaul and Italy proper. Everyone knew that if he led armed men across the Rubicon, it would plunge the Roman world into a civil war. According to the historian Suetonius, Caesar told his troops:

Despite knowing they would be starting a civil war, Caesar asked his men to follow him across the Rubicon River.

> *We may still draw back. But once across that little bridge, we shall have to fight*

it out. ... Let us ... follow where they [the gods] beckon, in vengeance on our double-dealing enemies. The die is cast!

As Caesar marched southward toward the capital, Rome fell into a state of near chaos. Caesar's opponents had not expected him to act so boldly and quickly. Ill prepared for a major fight, Pompey fled to Brundisium, in southeastern Italy. The consuls and many senators went with him. Thus, when Caesar and his soldiers entered Rome a few days later, they met no resistance.

Caesar forced his way into Rome's public treasury.

Still hoping to settle matters without major bloodshed, Caesar moved on to Brundisium. "I thought that

... I ought to go on trying for peace," Caesar wrote in his journal. "[So] I sent a member of my staff ... [to arrange] an interview with Pompey." But for unknown reasons, Pompey refused to talk. Not long afterward, he departed for Greece.

Returning to Rome, Caesar also tried to establish working relations with the remaining senators. In March, he met with the most respected of them, Marcus Tullius Cicero. Cicero was the finest and most famous orator in Rome. He had been one of the consuls during Catiline's conspiracy in 63 B.C., so Cicero and Caesar knew each other well.

The two men were usually on opposite sides of political issues, and this time it was no different. Cicero frankly informed Caesar that he felt obliged to back Pompey and the consuls. Later that day, Cicero wrote to a friend: "He asked me to think the matter over. ... I could not refuse. On that note we parted. So I imagine Caesar is not pleased with me." Not long afterward, Cicero joined Pompey in Greece.

It was not surprising, even to

Marcus Tullius Cicero (106–43 B.C.) is sometimes referred to as the last great champion of the Roman Republic. He distrusted military strongmen like Caesar and Pompey. And as they fought one another, he tried to hold the crumbling traditional government together. Cicero was highly educated and multitalented. A noted lawyer, orator, consul, senator, and writer, he left behind an enormous collection of writings. They include 58 long speeches, more than 800 letters, and 2,000 pages of essays on a wide range of subjects.

Caesar, that so many high-placed Romans took Pompey's side. First, Pompey was a great military hero who had never lost a battle. He had a massive power base in the eastern Mediterranean, with many loyal troops. In addition, Pompey enjoyed widespread support in parts of Spain, and he had control of most of Rome's navy.

To win the war, therefore, Caesar would have to fight on many fronts. He wasted no time in making the first move. While Pompey was getting organized in Greece, Caesar set out for Spain. In a mere two months, he forced Pompey's commanders there to surrender. Then Caesar rushed back to Rome and got the assembly to appoint him dictator. He claimed this was necessary to "save" Rome from Pompey.

Just a few days later, in January 48 B.C., Caesar gathered his forces and sailed for Greece. There, near the town of Pharsalus, the two armies faced off. Caesar had about 22,000 foot soldiers and 1,400 cavalry. Pompey's forces were considerably larger— at least 40,000 foot soldiers and about 7,000 horsemen. However, he was grossly overconfident. He told his officers that his cavalry would surprise Caesar's army by encircling it. This, Pompey claimed, would result in victory "before our troops have even thrown their javelins."

But when the two armies clashed on August 9, 48 B.C., Caesar was not fooled. He saw how Pompey had arranged his cavalry and guessed his opponent's plan. Caesar countered by ordering a unit of 3,000 of his own troops to move to a different spot. When Pompey's horsemen charged, that unit suddenly attacked them from the rear. It was Pompey's army that was surprised. Caesar won a resounding victory. He lost a mere 200 men, while an estimated 15,000 of Pompey's soldiers were killed.

Shocked and distressed, Pompey fled once more. This time he went to Egypt, where, he hoped, the local ruler would protect him. Caesar soon followed. At the time, neither man foresaw how dramatically his life was about to change.

Pompey's mention of his troops' throwing their javelins was a reference to standard Roman battle tactics. In his and Caesar's day, Roman soldiers formed battlefield units called cohorts. Each cohort was composed of about 480 men and roughly square-shaped. A general could order one or more cohorts to advance on the enemy. Or he could combine them into larger formations. He could also have the men in a cohort form a long line and charge. During a charge, the troops first hurled one of two javelins they carried. A few seconds later they threw the second. Then they drew their swords, crashed into the enemy lines, and began hacking away.

7 CAESAR AND CLEOPATRA

❧❧❧

Julius Caesar may have felt as though he was on a grand tour of the Mediterranean world. He had recently traveled from Italy to Spain, then back to Italy. From there he had hurried to Greece to fight Pompey. Now, in pursuit of his former father-in-law, Caesar headed for Egypt in 48 B.C.

Pompey had chosen Egypt as a refuge for two reasons. First, he looked on its young king, Ptolemy XIII, as a sort of friend. Pompey had once had business dealings with Ptolemy's father, Ptolemy XII, who was now dead. In addition, Egypt was rich in grain, gold, and ships. It was a good place to raise a new army to continue the war against Caesar.

But Pompey soon found that Egypt's boy king was far from a friend. Ptolemy's adult adviser, Pothinus,

Caesar was attracted to Cleopatra's physical charm, knowledge of politics, and ability to speak many languages.

saw Pompey's cause as hopeless. And fearing Caesar's wrath if Egypt helped Pompey, Pothinus urged Ptolemy to kill Pompey. The unsuspecting Roman general was stabbed to death in a small boat that was ferrying him ashore in northern Egypt.

Evidently Ptolemy and Pothinus thought Caesar would be grateful that they had rid him of

After Pompey's murder, Caesar, much to his disgust, was presented with the Roman general's head.

Pompey. But they were sorely mistaken. When Caesar arrived in Egypt, he was outraged over such brutal treatment of one of Rome's greatest heroes. Moreover, the Egyptian leaders were in for another unpleasant surprise. Caesar demanded that they pay him a large sum of money. He said he was collecting repayment of a loan that a wealthy Roman had given to Ptolemy XII, the young king's father.

While the Egyptians tried to decide how to respond, Caesar learned about the political situation in Egypt. There had been a power struggle after the death of Ptolemy XII, who had intended for his son and daughter Cleopatra to rule jointly. But the boy king and Pothinus had forced Cleopatra into exile. Caesar decided to end these civil conflicts. He wrote in his journal:

The second-century A.D. Greek historian Appian gave this account of Pompey's grisly murder: "A wretched little boat, with some of the [Egyptian] king's attendants on board, was sent out to Pompey. ... [He] was suspicious [because] the [Egyptian] king had neither come to meet him in person nor sent anyone important. ... [Suddenly a man in the boat] struck the first blow and the others followed. ... Pompey's head was cut off ... and someone buried the rest of the body on the shore."

The quarrel between the two rulers of Egypt affected the Roman people and consequently myself. ... I therefore made it known that I wished King Ptolemy and his

*Cleopatra
(69–30 B.C.)*

sister Cleopatra to disband their armies, to appear before me, and to settle their dispute in a legal way rather than by force of arms.

When Cleopatra learned that Caesar was in Egypt's capital, Alexandria, she hatched a plan to meet him in secret. She and a servant approached the palace after dark. The servant wrapped her in a sleeping bag. Then he smuggled her inside and into Caesar's quarters. "This little trick of Cleopatra's," Plutarch said, was "the first thing about her which captivated Caesar." Indeed, Caesar and Cleopatra quickly fell deeply in love. He was 52 and she was 21.

Caesar took Cleopatra's side in the ongoing struggle for the Egyptian throne. He had wanted her and her brother to try to get along. But Ptolemy, urged on by the power-hungry Pothinus, chose to fight.

Caesar had brought only a small number of troops with him to Egypt. They numbered just 3,200

foot soldiers and 800 horsemen. He sent for reinforcements. But until they arrived, he was greatly
outnumbered. Ptolemy's leading general, Achillas,
commanded 20,000 soldiers. "My own forces were

*Some accounts
say the smug-
gled Cleopatra
was wrapped
in a rug. Others
say it was a
laundry bag.*

The palace where Caesar stayed during his visit to Alexandria was huge and splendid. But it was only one of many wonders that Ptolemy I and his descendants had built there. These included a magnificent tomb to house the body of Alexander the Great; the largest library in the world, featuring more than 700,000 books; the Museum, a research center that attracted the world's leading scholars; and the Pharos, a lighthouse that towered to the then astounding height of 344 feet (105 m).

certainly not large enough," Caesar later recalled, "to fight a battle outside the city. All we could do, therefore, was to stay where we were and wait to see what Achillas intended to do."

By "where we were," Caesar meant the royal palace in Alexandria. Caesar had been staying there since his arrival and had many soldiers guarding him and Cleopatra. This made for a very strange situation. On one hand, though they controlled the palace, they were more or less trapped in it. On the other hand, their enemies, Ptolemy and Pothinus, were confined there, too. Thus, most of the opposing leaders in the coming war lived under the same roof. These uncomfortable circumstances lasted almost two months.

During that period, Achillas launched several attacks on the palace. But thanks to the skill and bravery of Caesar's soldiers, these assaults failed.

Achillas also tried to capture the Roman ships in the city's harbor. Caesar wrote in his journal: "The enemy realized that if they could gain possession of these ships … [they] would be able to cut me off from both reinforcements and supplies." To keep this from happening, Caesar ordered his men to burn the vessels.

The destruction of his own ships was only one of Caesar's unexpected and effective moves. He also ordered the execution of Pothinus. In addition, Caesar allowed Ptolemy to leave the palace and join Achillas. Caesar was planning to put Cleopatra on the throne as sole ruler of Egypt. Her people would better accept her, he foresaw, if Ptolemy died in battle

Plutarch wrote that when Caesar set his ships in Alexandria's harbor aflame, it caused the Great Library to catch fire. Modern historians, however, doubt the accuracy of this story.

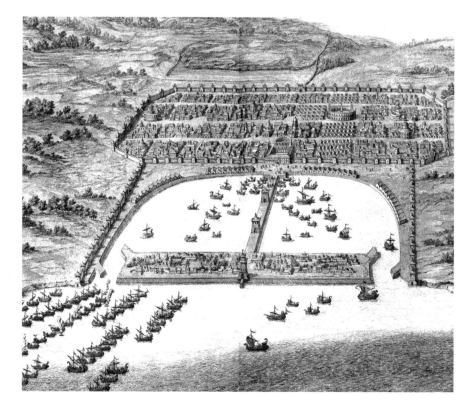

rather than as her and Caesar's captive.

This proved to be still another of Caesar's many shrewd political decisions. His reinforcements soon arrived in Egypt, and he and his forces left the city and joined them. In a battle in the nearby desert, the Romans easily crushed Achillas' army. Ptolemy lost his life, as Caesar had hoped he would. The boy king's body, decked out in golden armor, was found floating in the Nile.

On a trip up the Nile, Cleopatra's royal barge was joined by 400 other ships.

After his victory, Caesar saw to it that Cleopatra became queen. She was crowned in a splendid and solemn ceremony attended by all the Egyptian

nobles and priests. Cleopatra wanted to show her appreciation to her mentor and lover, so she took him on a voyage up the Nile. Caesar greatly enjoyed the trip, but after they returned to Alexandria, he had to leave. As Rome's self-appointed leader, he had to put down a rebellion in Asia Minor (what is now Turkey).

The lovers' parting was likely not a sad one. Caesar had made a new friend and ally whose support he could count on. And there was another connection between them that they may not yet have been aware of. As they said farewell, Cleopatra was pregnant with Caesar's child. ℘

HMP

8 FOUR MIGHTY TRIUMPHS

❧❦❧

During his stay in Egypt, Julius Caesar realized that his adventures there were little more than a side trip. True, Pompey had been defeated and killed. But the civil war was far from over. Pompey's able sons, Gnaeus and Sextus, still opposed Caesar. And they were joined by many senators and other leading Romans.

Before he could confront these enemies, however, Caesar had to deal with the trouble in Asia Minor. Rome had made many conquests there. Among them was the kingdom of Pontus, bordering the southern coast of the Black Sea. Recently the king of Pontus, Pharnaces II, had launched a revolt. In the process, his troops had murdered large numbers of Roman citizens.

After enjoying his trip with Cleopatra, Caesar once again returned to military campaigning.

Part of Caesar's job as dictator was to deal with such emergencies. Leaving Alexandria in June 47 B.C., he hurried northward. Soon he found Pharnaces at Zela, in eastern Asia Minor. The two armies made camp not far from each other, each atop a low hill.

The Romans were still strengthening their position when they noticed Pharnaces' troops leaving their own camp. At first Caesar thought his opponent was conducting a military drill. But then it became apparent that it was an all-out attack.

In the 40s B.C., Caesar traveled extensively throughout the Mediterranean.

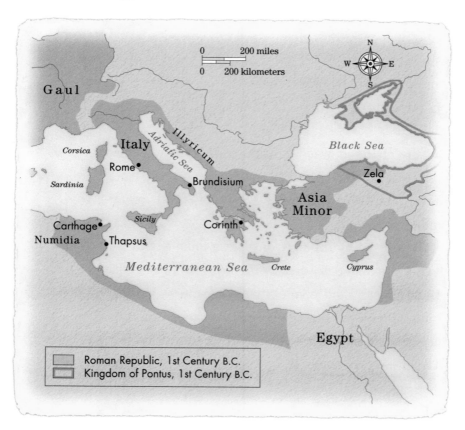

Things happened so fast that Caesar's troops barely had time to form proper battle lines. Still, they easily defeated the enemy, partly because Pharnaces was not a very good general. He had ordered his men to charge uphill at the Romans. That allowed Caesar's men to move downhill, giving them added power. Caesar's victory was so easy that he later described it in only three words: "Came, saw, conquered." This was his way of saying it was all in a day's work.

Returning to Italy in September, Caesar met with Cicero in Brundisium. When they had last talked, the senator had made it clear he was backing Pompey. But since Cicero had not fought in the great battle at Pharsalus, Caesar did not hold a grudge against him. In any case, Cicero was a skilled speaker and writer who might yet prove useful to him.

Cicero informed Caesar that government finances had fallen into a mess in the past year. The fault lay mainly with Caesar's high-ranking deputy, Marcus Antonius. Today he is better known as Mark Antony. While away in Egypt and Asia Minor, Caesar had left Antony in charge of Rome. But Antony was a heavy drinker and poor administrator. He also hated Cicero and had kept the senator from returning to Rome.

Caesar acted swiftly. First he punished Antony by barring him from holding public office for two years. Caesar also allowed Cicero to return to Rome. In addition, he began restoring financial order in the capital.

Caesar soon had to put his housecleaning on hold, however. Word came that Pompey's sons had massed a huge army in North Africa. Among their allies was the capable Roman general Quintus Metellus Scipio. The Pompeians also had the backing of the powerful senator Marcus Cato and Juba, ruler of the African kingdom of Numidia. In all, Caesar's enemies had about 80,000 foot soldiers, 20,000 to 30,000 cavalrymen, and close to 100 battle elephants.

Caesar's forces were far smaller. When he sailed for Africa, he had about 35,000 foot soldiers, 2,000 horsemen, and no elephants. But what Caesar lacked in manpower, he made up for in cunning. In April 46 B.C., he camped near Thapsus, a town on the coast of what is now Tunisia. Scipio, who was in command of the Pompeian forces, camped nearby. A few days later, Caesar led his army toward the enemy's position, near the sea. Scipio had lined up most of his soldiers and elephants in preparation for battle. But Caesar had earlier ordered some of his ships

Marcus Antonius (c. 82–30 B.C.), or Mark Antony, was long one of Caesar's closest associates. Antony joined the army in 57 B.C., when he was in his mid-20s. Three years later he acquired a key position on Caesar's staff in Gaul. Caesar liked him and gave him several important tasks. Antony led one part of Caesar's army in the battle of Pharsalus, for instance. The close relationship between the two men had major consequences later. Following Caesar's death, Antony became a chief contender in the power struggle for control of Roman lands.

to approach Scipio's camp from the seaward side. It appeared as if the vessels were going to land more of Caesar's troops there. He was only bluffing, but it worked.

Thinking they would soon be surrounded, many of Scipio's men panicked. As the Pompeian camp fell into confusion, Caesar's army attacked. According to an eyewitness account, he "spurred on his horse and charged the enemy's front." Meanwhile, many of his men attempted to slay Scipio's elephants:

The archers and slingers poured their eager javelins ... upon the elephants, and by the noise of their slings and stones, so terrified these animals, that turning upon their own men, they trod them down in heaps.

The Romans learned about using elephants in battle from the Greeks. It originated in India and spread to Greece through Persia.

The practice of using elephants in battle had advantages and disadvantages. One advantage was that one's elephants could trample enemy foot soldiers. Also, the beasts sometimes frightened enemy horses. A disadvantage of using elephants in war was that they might panic on the battlefield. When scared, they sometimes trampled their own soldiers. This happened to Scipio's men at Thapsus. By this time, using elephants in battle had become rare.

Caesar's troops continued to hold the upper hand, and most of Scipio's men soon fled. A while later they tried to surrender, but their opponents would not allow it. Filled with zeal because of their victory, Caesar's soldiers killed thousands of them. Scipio and Juba died fighting, and Cato committed suicide. While this slaughter was happening, Pompey's sons managed to escape and headed for Spain.

When Caesar returned to Rome in July 46 B.C., his reputation and authority were stronger than ever. Most of his political opponents now saw him as unbeatable. They gave up trying to resist him. In fact, many of the senators put on a great show trying to satisfy him. They appointed him dictator for 10 years and declared 40 days of public celebrations to honor his victories.

More important to Caesar, perhaps, was that he finally got the triumph he had been denied years before. Rome now staged four mighty triumphs for him, one after another. One honored his Gallic campaigns. The others celebrated his victories in Egypt, Asia Minor, and Africa. In the highlight of the Gallic

triumph, his former enemy, Vercingetorix, marched in chains. Caesar had kept him prisoner for six years solely for this purpose. Afterward, the defeated Gallic leader was executed.

In these moments of glory, Caesar was perhaps the most powerful person who had ever lived. He had big plans for Rome. And he looked forward to carrying them out in the years to come. He had no way of knowing that he would soon be dead. ❧

9 Chapter
DICTATOR FOR LIFE

ᕽᕽᕽ

Among the spectators at Julius Caesar's Egyptian triumph was Cleopatra. Caesar had invited her to spend some time with him in Rome. She brought their infant son with her. His name was Caesarion. Everyone knew he was Caesar's son. But to avoid embarrassment, Caesar did not admit this fact publicly. After all, he was still married to Calpurnia, an honorable Roman woman.

Cleopatra observed Caesar's attempt to make Rome more ordered and prosperous. It was clear that this was going to be a difficult task. During the civil war, many Romans, especially in the capital, had become unemployed. Idle and desperate, some of the jobless had turned to crime. Rome had become a less safe and less happy place to live.

The official name
of Caesar's son by
Cleopatra was Ptolemy
XV. But he was better
known by his informal
name, Caesarion. In
his biography of Caesar,
Suetonius wrote: "The
boy closely resembled
Caesar in features as
well as in gait [the way
he walked]." Caesar
admitted to some sena-
tors that the boy was
his, but he denied it in
public. One of Caesar's
friends even published
a book claiming that
Caesarion was not
Caesar's son.

Caesar attacked these problems with his usual boldness. He ordered the establishment of several new colonies. One would rise at Carthage, in North Africa. This was the site of a once great city the Romans had destroyed in the previous century. A second colony would be built at Corinth, in Greece. Corinth was another city the Romans had leveled in a past war. Another colony was to be at Hispalis, in southern Spain. More than 80,000 jobless Romans immediately moved to these new cities. This quickly reduced the unemployment and crime rates in Rome.

Caesar wanted to put many other reforms in place in Rome and across the empire. But for now he had to put these plans on hold. Once again, the trumpets of war were sounding, and he could not ignore them. Pompey's sons, Gnaeus and Sextus, had raised another army and seized large sections of Spain.

Hoping to end the long civil war once and for all, Caesar crossed to Spain. His forces numbered roughly 40,000 foot soldiers and 8,000 horsemen. Soon afterward, his great-nephew, Octavian, then

17, joined him in Spain. Caesar liked the young man and wanted to show him what a military expedition was like.

Caesar found the Pompeians near the town of Munda, in south-central Spain. Once again he was outnumbered. The enemy had between 70,000 and 80,000 men. Moreover, the Pompeians held an extremely well-fortified position.

Caesar saw no other choice but to launch a head-on attack. The battle, fought in March 45 B.C, was long, hard-fought, and bloody. "It was only with great difficulty," Plutarch wrote, that Caesar and his men "broke the enemy's resistance." In the end, more than 30,000 of the enemy lay dead. In what proved to be

When the Romans destroyed Corinth in 146 B.C., they first stole riches from the city.

Caesar's final battle, his losses were only about 1,000.

With the utter defeat of the last of Pompey's kin and allies, the civil war ended. Caesar returned to Rome in the fall of 45 B.C. Finally he could devote all of his energies to governing.

Getting right to work, Caesar made it clear how he intended to rule. He planned to make dramatic political and social changes. And he would produce these changes in the most efficient way possible. In his view, Rome's traditional republican system was out of date. It had too many public officials, worked too slowly, and got little done. It would be better, he argued, to have a single, very powerful ruler. Ideally that person would be fair and even-handed, and he would have the people's best interests at heart. Such an individual could get things done quickly and benefit everyone.

Caesar believed he was the right man for the job. As proof, he pointed to his recent success at reducing unemployment and crime. Now he proposed other changes that were equally sweeping and bold. Rome

At the height of his career, Caesar looked forward to reforming the Roman government.

should build several large canals across the empire, he said, to increase trade and commerce. Also, the number of slaves should be reduced. That would make more jobs available for free people.

In addition, Caesar argued, Rome's calendar needed to be overhauled. No one disagreed that it was cumbersome and inaccurate. Moving swiftly, he pushed this reform through. A version of the calendar he created is still widely used today.

Caesar's new ideas and governing style were quite popular. In particular, most members of the lower classes responded favorably. They were willing to give up some freedom in exchange for peace, jobs, security, and good government.

Opposition to Caesar came mainly from the upper classes. Members of the noble families were especially unhappy and, indeed, they had the most to lose from Caesar's reforms. They had long made up Rome's ruling class, and they resented having to do his bidding.

The mood of the dictator's opponents worsened in February

A major drawback of Rome's traditional calendar was that it followed the lunar (moon) cycle. At 355 days, it was 10¼ days shorter than the 365¼-day solar (sun) cycle. Over time, the two cycles did not match. That meant an annual event would occur earlier and earlier each year. Caesar hired a Greek astronomer named Sosigenes, who introduced a more reliable calendar with 365 days. To account for the extra quarter-day each year, he added an extra day every fourth year. That year is called a leap year.

44 B.C. About this time he began moving to obtain ultimate power. He had his supporters appoint him "dictator for life." Also, ugly rumors began to circulate. Some suggested that Caesar would declare himself king and conduct business from a golden throne.

*Marcus Brutus
(85–42 B.C.)*

A group of angry senators came to believe that it was their duty to save Rome from a tyrant. They were led by Marcus Brutus and Gaius Cassius. Their plan was to kill Caesar on March 15 in a chamber where the Senate was going to meet. The Romans called that date the ides of the month.

On that day the assassins struck. According to Suetonius:

> *As soon as Caesar took his seat, the conspirators crowded around him. ... One of the Casca brothers with a sweep of his dagger stabbed him just below the throat. ... He [Caesar] was leaping away when another dagger stabbed him just below the throat. ... Twenty-three dagger thrusts went home as he stood there.*

Fatally wounded, the dictator staggered and fell. Many of those present thought the spot where he landed was fitting. Caesar took his last breath while lying beneath a statue of his old enemy, Pompey.

Elated, the assassins ran into the street. They loudly proclaimed that they had restored liberty to the Roman people. But this was a mere illusion. They did not realize that the changes Caesar had set in motion could not be stopped. True, he was dead. But thanks in large part to him, the Roman Republic was doomed.

In his description of the murder, Plutarch said many of the assassins were injured by one another as they repeatedly stabbed Caesar.

10 CAESAR'S LEGACY— THE EMPIRE

☙❧

March 15, 44 B.C., marked a crucial turning point in Rome's history. On that day the mighty Gaius Julius Caesar met a brutal and untimely death. At first, most people were shocked into inaction. For perhaps an hour or more, no one even tried to move the blood-soaked body. "Caesar was left lying dead for some time," Suetonius recalled. Eventually, "three slave boys carried him home in a litter, with one arm hanging over the side." During the ongoing "state of confusion," as Plutarch put it, some people "bolted their doors." Others "left their counters and shops" and ran "to see the place where Caesar had been killed."

For a couple of days, Brutus, Cassius, and the other assassins were confident. They assumed that the Roman people would thank them for killing Caesar. They were sure the Republic would swiftly be restored. But their hopeful mood was short-lived. Mark Antony made the dead man's will public. When the people learned that Caesar had left a little money to every citizen, they began to turn on his killers. Soon mob violence erupted. "The people saw his body, all disfigured with his wounds," Plutarch said. In a fit of anger, "they ran to set fire to the houses of the murderers."

Most of the assassins managed to escape. Brutus and Cassius fled to Greece. They hoped to raise an army there to fight Antony, who had taken charge of Rome. But as it turned out, Antony was not the only powerful man they had to fear. The following year (43 B.C.), he joined forces with the 18-year-old Octavian. Caesar, to show his high regard for his grandnephew, wrote a will that adopted him as his son. This made Octavian Caesar's official heir. Antony now joined with Octavian and an influential general

Mark Antony (83–30 B.C.)

named Marcus Lepidus. Together they formed the Second Triumvirate.

The three men acted swiftly and brutally. They made lists of their political enemies and began killing them. At the top of Antony's list was Cicero. Antony's henchmen cut off Cicero's head and hands and hung them in Rome's main square. Large numbers of senators were killed, and the property of many more was seized. But the three men's thirst for power corrupted them. Antony and Octavian turned on Lepidus.

He spent the rest of his life under house arrest.

It was Antony and Octavian, therefore, who finally dealt with Caesar's killers. By the summer of 42 B.C., Brutus and Cassius had raised a large army. A huge battle took place at Philippi, in northern Greece. Antony and Octavian's army crushed the opposing forces. It was clear that the last hope of restoring the Republic was gone. Brutus and Cassius took their own lives.

The latest civil war had barely ended when another began. The remaining triumvirs were highly ambitious. Both Antony and Octavian wanted to occupy the office of dictator that Caesar had created in Rome. Moreover, each man saw himself as Caesar's

Brutus committed suicide by stabbing himself.

rightful heir. It was probably inevitable, therefore, that the two would compete to the death.

For a while, it looked as though Antony had the upper hand. He allied himself with Cleopatra, as Caesar had. Like Caesar, he became her lover. Cleopatra and Antony controlled most of Rome's eastern provinces. These were populous and rich in money, foodstuffs, and other resources. Octavian controlled Italy and the western provinces. He had fewer soldiers and less money than Antony. But Octavian was more cunning. He convinced many Romans that Antony was a traitor to his country. Cleopatra, he said, was an evil witch who wanted to be queen of Rome.

In the end, Octavian was victorious. The climax of the war was a major naval battle fought at Actium, in Greece, in 31 B.C. Antony and Cleopatra suffered a decisive defeat. After fleeing to Alexandria, they committed suicide.

These events left Octavian

Octavian's victory at Actium doomed Antony and Cleopatra's cause. At first glance, it appeared that they had the military advantage. They had 500 ships. Octavian had perhaps half that number. However, most of Antony's vessels were large, heavy, and slow. In contrast, Octavian's were smaller, faster, and more nimble. Octavian also had a very talented admiral—Marcus Agrippa—commanding his forces. Still another factor that worked in Octavian's favor was Antony's alliance with Cleopatra. In the midst of the battle, she turned and fled. Instead of staying and fighting on, Antony followed her. That ensured that his remaining ships and men would be defeated.

the most powerful person in the known world. The question for him was how to use that power. Like his adoptive father, Caesar, he believed Rome's republican system was no longer workable. Rule by a public-spirited dictator would be far more efficient. He realized that the Roman people were exhausted from decades of ruinous civil wars. They yearned for peace, stability, and security. To achieve these things, he thought, they might accept one-man rule.

Caesar had provided the basic blueprint for such rule. But he had made a costly mistake, Octavian realized. Caesar had viewed the republican system as his enemy. But the Romans, who respected tradition, were not yet ready to abandon that system.

Octavian (63 B.C.–14 A.D.)

Octavian wisely used the Republic to his advantage. Pretending to restore it, he kept the Senate and traditional public offices in place. Then, little by little, the senators and voters legally granted him immense powers. In addition, in 27 B.C. the Senate gave him a new name—Augustus, meaning "the revered one."

Augustus never called himself emperor, but he was one. And history came to see him as the first absolute dictator of a new and very different version of Rome. The mighty Roman Empire would rule the known world for five centuries. Caesar's role in the empire's creation was never forgotten. Beginning with Augustus, who called himself Augustus Caesar, every emperor used the name Caesar as an honorary title. In a way, Julius Caesar achieved in death the ultimate power he aggressively sought in life. ℘

The Senate and Roman people bestowed many powers and honors on Augustus. But as Roman historians told it, he remained humble. He claimed he had no interest in achieving wealth or glory for himself. Instead he was dedicated to running the realm fairly and effectively. "May I be privileged to build firm and lasting foundations for the Government," he said, according to Suetonius. "May I also ... [carry] with me, when I die, the hope that these foundations which I have established for the State will abide secure."

CAESAR'S LIFE

100 B.C.

Born in Rome

84 B.C.

Marries Cornelia, daughter of the popular politician Cornelius Cinna

75 B.C.

Captured by pirates; after paying a ransom and gaining his freedom, he returns and arrests them

100 B.C.

100 B.C.

Use of paper developed in China

82 B.C.

Sulla becomes dictator of Rome

WORLD EVENTS

65 B.C.

Holds the post of aedile, an official who maintains public buildings and supervises public markets and games; stages large gladiator fights

69 B.C.

Wins election to the post of quaestor, a public official in charge of financial affairs

63 B.C.

Elected praetor, a court judge; gains prominence by trying to persuade the Senate to imprison rather than execute a group of traitors

65 B.C.

73 B.C.

Slave revolt of Spartacus begins; the slave army is defeated in 71 B.C.

CAESAR'S LIFE

59 B.C.

Serves as consul; by the end of his term, is appointed governor of the two Gauls and Illyricum

60 B.C.

Invites the noted politicians Pompey and Crassus to join him in an informal alliance later called the First Triumvirate; wins election as consul for the following year

58 B.C.

Launches a conquest of Transalpine Gaul (now northern France and Belgium)

60 B.C.

60 B.C.

The Seleucid Kingdom comes to an end with the murder of the last two emperors on orders from Rome

58 B.C.

Cyprus becomes a Roman province

WORLD EVENTS

57 B.C.

Defeats the Belgae, tribesmen inhabiting northern Gaul

55–54 B.C.

Leads two invasions of Britain, both of which fail

52 B.C.

Attacks the Gallic fortress of Alesia during a major rebellion of the Gallic tribes

55 B.C.

54 B.C.

Pompey builds the first permanent theater in Rome

52 B.C.

Lutetia, the future city of Paris, France, is built

Caesar's Life

48 B.C.

Decisively defeats Pompey at Pharsalus, in Greece; travels to Egypt in pursuit of Pompey; involves himself in a power struggle between the Egyptian king and the king's sister, Cleopatra

49 B.C.

Crosses the Rubicon River, sending the Roman realm into civil war

47 B.C.

Installs Cleopatra on Egypt's throne

50 B.C.

50 B.C.

The Maya city of Cerros is built with a complex of temples and ball courts; it was abandoned 100 years later for unknown reasons

48 B.C.

Yuan becomes emperor of China's Han dynasty

World Events

45 B.C.

As dictator of Rome, orders a major revision of the calendar

46 B.C.

Defeats his remaining enemies; returns to Rome and takes part in four huge triumphs

44 B.C.

Assassinated by a group of senators on March 15, the Ides of March

45 B.C.

40 B.C.

Herod the Great is appointed King of Judea by the Romans

DATE OF BIRTH: July 13, 100 B.C.

BIRTHPLACE: Rome, Italy

FATHER: Gaius Julius Caesar

MOTHER: Aurelia

FIRST SPOUSE: Cornelia,

DATE OF MARRIAGE: 84 B.C.

CHILD: Julia (c. 83–54 B.C.)

SECOND SPOUSE: Pompeia

DATE OF MARRIAGE: 68 B.C.

THIRD SPOUSE: Calpurnia

DATE OF MARRIAGE: 59 B.C.

OTHER CHILDREN: Caesarion (47–30 B.C.),
with Cleopatra
Octavian (63 B.C.–14 A.D.),
by adoption

DATE OF DEATH: March 15, 44 B.C.

PLACE OF CREMATION: Rome's main Forum

Further Reading

Forsyth, Fiona. *Cicero: Defender of the Republic.* New York: Rosen, 2003.

Kamm, Antony. *Julius Caesar.* New York: Routledge, 2006.

Kebric, Robert B. *Roman People.* Boston: McGraw-Hill, 2005.

Malam, John. *Gladiator: Life and Death in Ancient Rome.* New York: Dorling Kindersley, 2002.

McCaughrean, Geraldine. *Roman Myths.* New York: Margaret McElderry Books, 2001.

Nardo, Don. *From Founding to Fall: A History of Rome.* San Diego: Lucent Books, 2003.

Platt, Richard. *Julius Caesar: Great Dictator of Rome.* London: Dorling Kindersley, 2001.

Look for more Signature Lives
books about this era:

Alexander the Great: *World Conqueror*

Aristotle: *Philosopher, Teacher, and Scientist*

Confucius: *Chinese Philosopher and Teacher*

Hatshepsut: *Egypt's First Female Pharaoh*

Hypatia: *Mathematician, Inventor, and Philosopher*

Ramses II: *Egyptian Pharaoh, Warrior, and Builder*

Socrates: *Ancient Greek in Search of Truth*

Thucydides: *Ancient Greek Historian*

ON THE WEB

For more information on this topic,
use FactHound.

1. Go to *www.facthound.com*
2. Type in this book ID: 0756538343
3. Click on the *Fetch It* button.

FactHound will find the best
Web sites for you.

HISTORIC SITES

Alesia Museum and Excavations
21550 Alise-Sainte-Reine
France
33 38096 1095
Artifacts and reconstructions of the great
battle Caesar fought against the Gauls at
Alesia, now the town of Alise-Sainte-Reine

Roman Forum
Via dei Fori Imperiali
Rome, Italy
39 06699 0110
The ruins of Rome's famous main
square, including a reconstruction of
the Senate House

aedile
in the Roman Republic, a public official in
charge of maintaining buildings and supervising
public games

alliance
agreement between nations or groups of people to
work together

consul
in the Roman Republic, one of two administrator-
generals who jointly ran the government; their
office was called the consulship

coup
sudden change in government, often by force

creditor
person who lends someone money and expects
to be paid back

dictator
in the Roman Republic, a public official who ran
the government during a national emergency

in absentia
Latin term meaning doing something in
one's absence

legate
commander of a Roman legion

legion
Roman military regiment having about 5,000 men

optimates
political group that opposed the populares in the
Roman Republic

orator
someone skilled at public speaking

patricians
members of a group of ancient noble Roman families

plebs
common people in ancient Rome

plunder
valuable items stolen during acts of war

populares
political group that opposed the optimates in the Roman Republic

praetor
high-ranking court judge in the Roman Republic

quaestor
public financial officer in the Roman Republic

republican
having to do with the Republic, the representative government that ruled Rome from about 509 to 27 B.C.; that time period is also referred to as the Republic

Senate
Rome's oldest and most powerful legislative body

tribune
junior officer in the Roman army

triumph
splendid parade to honor a victorious general

triumvirate
three people in ancient Rome who ruled jointly

Chapter 1

Page 11, line 14: Julius Caesar. *War Commentaries of Caesar.* Trans. Rex Warner. New York: New American Library, 1987, p. 173.

Page 12, sidebar: Ibid.

Page 13, line 8: Ibid., p. 177.

Page 14, line 4: Ibid., p. 178.

Page 14, lines 17 and 25: Ibid., p. 180.

Chapter 2

Page 22, sidebar: Suetonius. *Lives of the Twelve Caesars,* published as *The Twelve Caesars.* Trans. Robert Graves, rev. Michael Grant. New York: Penguin, 2003, p. 34.

Page 22, line 26, Ibid., p. 14.

Page 24, line 5: Plutarch. *Fall of the Roman Republic: Six Lives By Plutarch.* Trans. Rex Warner. New York: Penguin, 2006, p. 246.

Page 24, line 26: Ibid., p. 245.

Chapter 3

Page 30, sidebar: *Fall of the Roman Republic: Six Lives By Plutarch,* p. 248.

Page 32, line 6: Ibid.

Page 32, line 10: Ibid., p. 249.

Page 32, line 15: Ibid., p. 248.

Chapter 4

Page 38, line 18: *Fall of the Roman Republic: Six Lives By Plutarch,* p. 254.

Page 39, line 8: Grant, Michael. *Julius Caesar.* New York: M. Evans, 1992, p. 29.

Page 42, line 14: *Lives of the Twelve Caesars,* p. 21.

Chapter 5

Page 46, line 27: Ibid., p. 22.

Page 49, sidebar: *War Commentaries of Caesar,* p. 11.

Page 50, line 1: Ibid., p. 23–24.

Page 51, sidebar: Ibid., p. 47.

Chapter 6

Page 56, line 24: Ibid., pp. 214, 216.

Page 57, line 10: *Lives of the Twelve Caesars,* p. 28.

Page 58, line 13: *War Commentaries of Caesar,* p. 226.

Page 59, line 22: Cicero. *Letters to Atticus.* 4 vols. Trans. D.R. Shackleton Bailey. New York: Cambridge University Press, 1978, vol. 3, p. 97.

Page 60, line 25: *War Commentaries of Caesar,* p. 320.

Chapter 7

Page 65, line 24: Ibid., p. 330.

Page 65, sidebar: Appian. *The Civil Wars.* Trans. John Carter. New York: Penguin, 1996, p. 114.

Page 66, line 17: *Fall of the Roman Republic: Six Lives By Plutarch,* p. 290.

Page 67, line 4: *War Commentaries of Caesar,* p. 331.

Page 68, line 27: Ibid., p. 332.

Chapter 8

Page 75, line 8: *Fall of the Roman Republic: Six Lives By Plutarch,* p. 292.

Page 77, line 8: Julius Caesar. *The African War.* 25 Jan. 2008. The Literature Network http://www.online-literature.com/caesar/africanwar/3, p. 4.

Chapter 9

Page 82, sidebar: *Lives of the Twelve Caesars,* p. 36.

Page 83, line 11: *Fall of the Roman Republic: Six Lives By Plutarch,* p. 296.

Page 86, line 22: *Lives of the Twelve Caesars,* p. 50.

Chapter 10

Page 89, line 6: Ibid., p. 51.

Page 89, line 10: *Fall of the Roman Republic: Six Lives By Plutarch,* pp. 306–307.

Page 90, line 7: Ibid., p. 308.

Page 95, sidebar: *Lives of the Twelve Caesars,* p. 69.

Appian. *The Civil Wars*. Trans. John Carter. New York: Penguin, 1996.

Bradford, Ernle. *Julius Caesar: The Pursuit of Power*. New York: Morrow, 1984.

Caesar, Julius. *Commentary on the Gallic War*, in *War Commentaries of Caesar*. Trans. Rex Warner. New York: New American Library, 1987.

Dio Cassius. *Roman History*, excerpted in *The Roman History: The Reign of Augustus*. Trans. Ian Scott-Kilvert. New York: Penguin, 1987.

Cicero. *Letters to Atticus*. 4 vols. Trans. D.R. Shackleton Bailey. New York: Cambridge University Press, 1978.

Everitt, Anthony. *Cicero: The Life and Times of Rome's Greatest Politician*. New York: Random House, 2001.

Fuller, J.F.C. *Julius Caesar: Man, Soldier, and Tyrant*. Cambridge, Mass.: Da Capo, 1991.

Goldsworthy, Adrian. *Caesar: Life of a Colossus*. New Haven, Conn.: Yale University Press, 2006.

Grant, Michael. *Julius Caesar*. New York: M. Evans, 1992.

Holland, Tom. *Rubicon: The Last Years of the Roman Republic*. New York: Anchor, 2005.

Jimenez, Ramon L. *Caesar Against Rome: The Great Roman Civil War*. Westport, Conn.: Praeger, 2000.

Langguth, A.J. *A Noise of War: Caesar, Pompey, Octavian and the Struggle for Rome*. New York: Simon and Schuster, 1994.

Matyszak, Philip. *Chronicle of the Roman Republic*. New York: Thames and Hudson, 2003.

Meier, Christian. *Caesar*. Trans. David McLintock. New York: HarperCollins, 2004.

Plutarch. *Life of Caesar*, in *Fall of the Roman Republic: Six Lives By Plutarch*. Trans. Rex Warner. New York: Penguin, 2006.

Sallust. *The Jugurthine War/The Conspiracy of Catiline*. Trans. S.A. Handford. New York: Penguin, 1988.

Suetonius. *Lives of the Twelve Caesars*, published as *The Twelve Caesars*. Trans. Robert Graves, rev. Michael Grant. New York: Penguin, 2003.

Taylor, Lily Ross. *Party Politics in the Age of Caesar*. Berkeley: University of California Press, 1984.

Yavetz, Zwi. *Julius Caesar and His Public Image*. Ithaca, N.Y.: Cornell University Press, 1983.

Historian and award-winning writer Don Nardo has published many volumes about the ancient world, among them *Life in Ancient Athens*, *Life of a Roman Gladiator*, *Egyptian Mythology*, *Empires of Mesopotamia*, *The Etruscans*, literary companions to the works of Homer, Sophocles, and Euripides, and the *Greenhaven Encyclopedia of Greek and Roman Mythology*. He lives with his wife, Christine, in Massachusetts.

Image Credits